WARREN PULLEY

Ku Klux Kalifornia

Contents

1

Ku Klux Kalifornia and Racism

Racism is an ugly and pervasive reality in many parts of the world, one that has caused untold suffering, injustice, and death. Racism is based on the belief that certain races are superior to others, which results in the oppression of those who do not fit into the accepted social hierarchy. This type of discrimination takes many forms, including prejudice, violence, segregation, and economic disadvantages. It can manifest itself in subtle ways such as a refusal to hire or promote people based on their race, or it may be overt such as physical attacks against members of certain ethnicity. No matter how it appears, racism is an abhorrent practice that must be addressed if we are to create a more just and equitable society.

To combat racism, it is important to first recognize and understand its root causes. In most cases, these are linked to a lack of understanding between different cultures and backgrounds. Education can be used as an effective tool for promoting awareness and understanding, while legislation can help to protect people from discrimination in the workplace or in other areas of life. Additionally, individuals can work together to create positive change in their own community by challenging any forms of racism they encounter and promoting diversity. Together, we can all strive to build a world that is free from the oppression and suffering caused by racism.

It is also important to remember that racism is a problem experienced by members of all races and ethnicity. People of color have been the primary victims of racism, but there are instances where white people too have been targeted or discriminated against. This type of discrimination often goes unrecognized or ignored in our society, leaving those affected feeling isolated and powerless. We must challenge this type of racism just as we do other forms, in order to create a world where everyone is treated with respect and dignity.

Finally, it is important that we continue the fight against racism on an ongoing basis. This means being aware of current events that involve issues of race and taking action when necessary. It also means being open to learning more about different cultures and perspectives, in order to expand our understanding of the world. We must recognize that racism is a systemic problem that requires collective effort and commitment if we are to create lasting change.

Racism has caused untold suffering throughout history, but there is still hope for a better future. By working together to create a more just and equitable world, we can make sure that everyone is treated with respect and dignity. Let us stand united in the fight against racism—for only then can we truly achieve true justice for all.

2

Ku Klux Klan Facts In America and California

In the tumultuous period of Reconstruction following the Civil War, former Confederate soldiers formed a sinister organization the Ku Klux Klan.

This first iteration was devoted to white supremacy and instilling fear in African Americans throughout southern states. At its peak during 1870s, it wreaked havoc on local communities before ultimately dying down by decade's end.

However this would not be their last act as tensions once again boiled over near century mark with renewed membership reaching four million members across the United States- from rural south all way up to west coast cities -by 1920 marking an all time high for KKK activity in America.

The History of Klan activities in California stretch from early 1868 until this very day.

California Klan Activities in the 1860's

In spring 1868 Ku Klux Klan members raided ranches in Northern California then captured and savagely beat the Chinese workers

In April 1869, a Ku Klux Klan proclamation, reported the Patriot of San Jose, threatened the destruction of all the crops of persons employing even a single China man in the San Jose Valley

1869, suspected Ku Klux Klan arsonists burned down a Methodist church in the San Jose valley that operated as a Sunday school for Chinese children

April 1869 the Ku Klux Klan reportedly again threatened to disembowel a private citizen near Marysville, California, for his progressive views on race

4

California Klan Activities in The 1920's

1922 Ku Klux Klan members become highly active in Inglewood, California

October 1923 the Lodi Sentinel reports highly organized Klan activity in Lodi California

1922active branch of the K.K.K. in San Diego was the Exalted Cyclops of San Diego No. 64

1920s, there was a big KKK rally where Glendale's Community College

Ku Klux Klan expands membership in 1920s Lodi California

1922 the Los Angeles Police Chief Louis D. Oaks outed as a Klan member

April 5, 1924 6,000 Klan members hold a rally in Stocktons Oak Park near Lodi, CA

August 1923 40 Klan members are initiated into the Ku Klux Klan In Lodi California

The resurgence of Klan activity is reported by in San Diego California in the

1920s

May 4, 1922 the Long Beach Press out's many Long Beach Police Officers as Klan members

1922 the Los Angeles County Sheriff William Taeger outed as a Klan member

Nov. 18, 1924, Long Beach Police Officers hold a mock lynching of three Black illegally detained teenagers

In 1926, the California Klan's annual convention was held in Long Beach

In 1927 Klan members Oscar Hauge, who was elected as Long Beach City Mayor

John Porter thrived as Klan leader and became mayor of Los Angeles in 1928

1924–1936 Five of Brea Californias first (8) mayors were Ku Klux Klansmen as were six of the ten councilmen who sat on the board of trustees from 1924 to 1936

Aug. 2, 1924 a very large Klan rally near is held in St. Helena California

In the 1920 Fullerton California's Moore, Municipal Judge French and schools Superintendent were all members of the Ku Klux Klan as well as (7) of its first (18) city councilmen members of the Klan from 1918-1930.

In 1924, four Klan members were elected to the Anaheim city council

July 29th, 1924 Anaheim held one of the largest Klan gatherings ever held in California

1924 Fullerton holds a large open air Ku Klux Klan rally

May 24 1924 50,000 people attend Klan Rally in Fresno County Fair

May of 1924 Klansman held rallys in (4) of Downey California's largest churches

In 1925 Klansman G.W. Price, plots to rid Los Angeles three black leaders by involving them in a traffic accident and having them unfairly convicted

5

Racism Is A National Shame

Racism is wrong because it violates the fundamental principles of human rights, equality, and dignity. It denies people their basic right to be treated as equals regardless of their skin color, religion, or cultural background. Racism creates a hierarchy in which some groups are seen as superior to others and are given more power, resources, and opportunity than those deemed inferior. This unequal distribution of power and privilege can lead to countless forms of discrimination that can have serious impacts on individuals' lives.

At an individual level, racism can cause psychological harm by making people feel less worthy or more ashamed about their identity. It also perpetuates negative stereotypes about different racial groups, which serves to further entrench racially biased attitudes and beliefs within society. These stereotypes can cause people to be viewed differently in terms of employment opportunities, quality housing, education access, healthcare services and other areas essential for leading a successful life. Racism can create a system where certain racial groups are excluded from enjoying the same privileges as others because they are denied a fair chance at success.

On a broader societal level, racism undermines the collective spirit needed for social cohesion and justice across racial groups. It has been linked to race-based violence such as hate crimes as well as structural injustices including mass incarceration rates among minorities relative to white populations. Ultimately, racism leads to feelings of alienation among radicalized communities and contributes to systemic inequalities that marginalize them further from mainstream society.

It's important for us all to recognize that racism has very real consequences even when it isn't expressed explicitly through verbal or physical abuse but rather through more subtle discriminatory practices such as implicit bias or microaggressions. We must strive for greater understanding for our differences just as much as we should strive for greater tolerance for them if we hope create a society that is truly inclusive of everyone regardless of their background or identity.

6

California Klan Activities in The 1930's

The Klan had a chapter in Inglewood as late as October 1931

During the 1930s, the California Ku Klux Klan groups merge with racist groups such as the MinuteMen, and White Guards

1930 to 1931, the San Diego Ku Klux Klan greatly expanded

7

California Klan Activities in The 1940's

The 1940s saw major growth of Ku Klux Klan membership throughout California, with the Klan located in Los Angeles serving as its western headquarters

Klan suspected of blowing up young black families home December 16, 1945

8

California Klan Activities in The 1960's

The Klan holds a member reactivation rally in Soledad Canyon on September 17, 1966.

9

California Klan Activities in The 1970's

During the 1970 the Ku Klux Klan openly operated at U.S. Marine Corp Base Camp Pendleton

1970s, Tom Metzger, emerged as California's new Klan leader

How Does Religion Play A Role In Racism

Religion has always been a significant factor in racism, as it is often used to justify or rationalize discriminatory or oppressive beliefs and behaviors. Religion can be used to propagate ideas of racial superiority or inferiority, and it can be used to promote fear and hatred of those deemed "different." In some cases, religious teachings are used to reinforce existing inequalities between different racial groups. For example, some Christian denominations use passages from the Bible to support the idea that certain races are superior over others. This kind of thinking has been used throughout history to support the oppression of black people in many parts of the world.

Even in modern societies, religion plays a role in racism. In America, for instance, certain sects of Christianity have been found to cause rifts between different ethnic groups. The Black Lives Matter movement has faced opposition from certain religious figures who believe that police brutality and systemic racism aren't issues that need attention or change. Similarly, bigotry against LGBTQ+ people is justified with religious ideals and scripture instead of logical arguments grounded in social justice.

In addition to using religion for justification for racism, modern-day white supremacists also utilize religious symbolism as a way to spread their own message of hate and exclusion. They use terms such as "racial purity" which suggest that one's identity should be determined solely by their race—a core belief among many white supremacists. Moreover, these individuals often adopt symbols like crosses and swastikas as part of their brand because they invoke strong feelings about faith and heritage within the crowd they seek to target with their hateful messages.

When examining how religion contributes to racism today, it's important not only to consider what is explicitly stated in scriptures but also how certain interpretations can lead to oppressive behavior towards minority communities. By understanding how white supremacy seeks out religious elements that confirm its belief system, we can work together towards a more inclusive society where everyone is welcome regardless of background or beliefs.

11

California Klan Activities in The 1980's

November 1981 the Ku Klux Klan Imperial Highway and Firestone Boulevard then distributed racist Klan fliers

In 1982 the Ku Klux Klan formally requested recognition from the City Council to move into the City of Downey California

On December 10, 1983, the Klan boasted of beheading undocumented aliens

In 1980 San Diego and Oceanside declared the Ku Klux Klan was stockpiling weapons allegedly preparing for the race war

December 9, 1989 police officer, Douglas K. Seymour, testified that the Ku KLux Klan in San Diego County remained one of the strongest chapters in the United States

12

California Klan Activities in 2016

July 2016 Racist Klan Fliers are posted in San Francisco's upper Haight district

13

California Klan Activities in 2017

April 2017 White Nationalists Klan groups involved in violent physical altercation in Berkeley CA

14

California Klan Activities in 2018

August 13 2018 the Ku Klux Klan post racists fliers in Suisun City located in Solano County California

15

What Does Racism Mean For Children

Racism can have a profoundly negative impact on children, as it can lead to a range of physical and psychological issues. Racism can cause children to feel devalued and isolated due to being subjected to discriminatory treatment or verbal abuse. This can lead to lasting feelings of inferiority, which may impede the child's ability to fully engage in society and form healthy relationships with others. The short-term effects of racism on children include decreased academic performance, increased school avoidance and truancy, difficulties forming peer relationships, higher levels of depression, anxiety, and stress, as well as increased risk for developing physical health problems such as hypertension. Long-term impacts include lower self-esteem, poorer educational outcomes, decreased job prospects and career opportunities (due to continued discrimination), difficulty forming meaningful relationships with others (due to feelings of distrust or wariness), and further mental health issues such as complex post-traumatic stress disorder (PTSD).

For many young people who are subject to racism from a young age, the effects can become deeply entrenched in their identities. Children who witness or experience racism may internalize these experiences leading them to believe that they are inferior or undeserving of respect due to their race or ethnicity. They may be more likely than their peers without such experiences to disconnect from people around them by avoiding social interactions out of fear of being judged negatively due to their race or ethnicity. In addition, these experiences may contribute towards poorer life outcomes overall; for example, individuals who experience racism during childhood are more likely than those who do not experience racism at an early age to have lower levels of education attainment and socioeconomic status later in life compared with their peers without such experiences.

In order for societies across the world to create equitable environments where all children can grow up free from racism it is crucial that adults take action at all levels - both individually and collectively -to address racism when it occurs first-hand and work together towards fostering anti-racist values within our communities. This means putting in place laws that promote equal rights for all regardless of ethnicity or racial identity; providing access to education about bias, privilege and power dynamics so that youth understand how racism has been systemically embedded into our cultures; engaging conversations about race with family members; making sure your workplace is equitable for everyone regardless of race; speaking out against any forms of inequality; standing up against discrimination when witnessing it unfold before you; supporting organizations/groups working on behalf of marginalized communities; using language that challenges racist stereotypes; educating yourself on the history and continuing dynamics of oppression faced by various racial/ethnic groups around the globe; pushing back against media representations which perpetuate damaging stereotypes about certain racial/ethnic groups; actively listening when someone shares an experience related to racism rather than dismissing it out of hand; recognizing your own privileges associated with your racial identity etc.

16

California Klan Activities in 2020

January 1 2020 Klan member spread racists fliers in the city of Tulelake California

May 3, 2020 A man wearing a Ku Klux Klan hood shops in a local San Diego grocery store

September 18 2020 San Leandro California City Council classifies the Ku Klux Klan a domestic terrorist group

17

California Klan Activities in 2021

APRIL 9, 2021 Ku Klux Klan m members promote White Lives Matter in Huntington Beach, and distribute Ku Klux Klan fliers in Newport Beach and Huntington Beach California

18

Society And Its Fight Against Racism

Society should fight back against racist groups by recognizing the problem at hand and taking active steps to counteract it. This could include implementing more education programs that focus on respect and understanding through empathy, as well as actively engaging with members of affected communities to better understand their needs and concerns. Additionally, those in positions of power (such as politicians, business leaders, and educators) should be vocal in denouncing racism and discrimination and should use their influence to lead by example.

At the same time, legislation must be passed that works towards eliminating discriminatory practices within both public and private sectors. This could include creating laws or policies that prohibit workplace racism or discrimination based on race, gender, religion, nationality or any other factor. Furthermore, anti-discrimination laws must be strictly enforced so that those who violate them are held accountable for their actions.

Moreover, governments should provide appropriate funding for grassroots campaigns against racism in all its forms; this could involve supporting community organizations that work towards equality or providing legal aid to victims of racial discrimination. Social media can also play an important role in combating bigotry and hatred; platforms such as Facebook and Twitter should take steps to limit hate speech while encouraging constructive dialogue between different ethnicities and social classes.

Finally, individuals must take a stand against racism whenever they encounter it——whether in person or online——and speak out without fear of retribution; only then will we truly start to make progress towards a fairer future for our society.

19

List of Hate Groups Active In California

A

- ACT for America
- American Freedom Alliance
- American Freedom Party
- American Nazi Party
- American Vanguard
- As-Sabiqun

B

- Bare Naked Islam
- Black Riders Liberation Party

C

- California Skinheads
- Californians for Population Stabilization
- Chalcedon Foundation
- Chick Publications
- Christian Anti-Defamation Commission
- Committee for Open Debate on the Holocaust
- Counter Jihadist Coalition of Southern California
- Counter-Currents Publishing
- Crew 38

D

- David Horowitz Freedom Center

E

- European-American Evangelistic Crusades

G

- Gallows Tree Wotansvolk Alliance
- Golden State Skinheads

H

- Hate Crime Streetwear Productions
- Holy Nation of Odin

I

- Identity Evropa
- Institute for Historical Review
- Islamthreat.com
- Israel United In Christ
- Israelite School of Universal Practical Knowledge

J

- Jewish Defense League
- Jihad Watch

L

- Loyal White Knights of the Ku Klux Klan

M

- Masjid al Islam
- Mass Resistance California

N

- Nation of Islam
- National Coalition for Immigration Reform (formerly CCIR)
- New Black Panther Party
- Noble Breed Kindred

O

- Occidental Observer
- Official Street Preachers
- OMNI Christian Book Club

P

- Pacific Coast Knights of the Ku Klux Klan
- Pacific Justice Institute

R

- Ruth Institute

S

- Sacto Skins
- Save California
- Sicarii 1715
- Soldiers of Odin

T

- The Daily Stormer
- The Realist Report
- Tony Alamo Christian Ministries
- Tradition in Action
- Traditional Values Coalition
- Traditionalist Worker Party

U

- United Northern and Southern Knights of the Ku Klux Klan

V

- Verity Baptist Church
- Vinland Clothing
- Vinlanders Social Club

W

- Western Hammerskins

20

How The Human Race Should Work To End Racism

In closing, teaching racial tolerance and acceptance is essential for the growth of a healthy and prosperous society. It is imperative that individuals from all backgrounds recognize their own biases and strive to create a positive environment where human diversity and inclusion are celebrated. By learning about the different cultures, customs, and values of our fellow citizens, we can understand each other better and further develop our empathy towards one another. This knowledge can also help us build mutual respect and understanding between members of different racial or ethnic groups.

Furthermore, by creating social support networks to combat racism, we can help prevent discrimination in the workplace, educational institutions, public settings, law enforcement agencies, media outlets and other areas of life where disparities exist. Enforcing anti-racist policies in these areas is paramount in order to ensure that everyone has an equal opportunity to succeed in life regardless of skin color or ancestry.

In addition to these measures, it is important that society encourages open dialogue between its citizens on race-related issues so that people can work together towards making our world a more tolerant place for all.

www.ingramcontent.com/pod-product-compliance
Lightning Source LLC
Chambersburg PA
CBHW071553260726

48653CB00008BA/3134